I0474251

First published by J. Michael Stattelman

CONTENTS

DEDICATION:

This book is dedicated to the Lord God above for providing me the experiences that allowed me to learn as I grew and to my kids, nieces and nephews. Maya, Aaron, Blake, Maci, Chase, Kali, MaKenzi and Søren. Katelyn, Kameron, Kylie, Kennedy, Kaden and Kira. Jayden, Saraya, and Lyrah. I love you all more than I will ever be able to show or tell you. It has been my goal to not only provide you with life opportunities, guidance and fun. In doing so be an example to you for education and what a productive, happy successful life you can have whenever you want. It will require you to put forth the maximum effort and then put forth even more, keep a never quit attitude and gather all of the knowledge to back it up. I assure you, that success will be yours.

Best wishes always,
Dad/Uncle Mike

"You are either a consumer or you are a producer, you either add value or you subtract from it. It really is that black and white!"

MJS

INTRODUCTION:

This book is for anyone tasked with leadership in any capacity of an Information technology team, unit, department or company. Whether you are a CIO, CTO, Director, Supervisor, Manager, Program/Project manager, Architect, Engineer, Tech lead, Business Analyst, Test lead, Data scientist, Data modeler, DBA, Developer or Tester. Whether you work in Management, Analytics, Operations, Marketing, Software, Hardware, Networking, Accounting, Social Media, Help Desk, Sales, Healthcare, Manufacturing, Financial Services, Pharmaceuticals, Retail, Food Service, Staffing or Compliance and want better. The strategies and tactics herein are proven to make things happen if you apply them.

This is not hyperbole; this is not industry jargon or regurgitated talking points, if you want to be more efficient, more effective, more productive or just flat out #MORE from a leadership and leadership capability perspective, this book is for you.

I decided on the term Meta for the following reasons: Merriam-Webster defines Meta as the following: more comprehensive: transcending

<metapsychological> —usually used with the name of a discipline to designate a new but related discipline designed to deal critically with the original one <metamathematics>. I was primarily focused on the "more-comprehensive: transcending" aspects of the word. I was also partial to the part that highlighted "To deal critically with the original one". I think there is really no comprehensive IT leadership book available that is as tuned in as necessary or one that offers an approach that can be used across industries with the adaptable nature as is required. My goal for the readers of this book is to push the standards of leadership higher and higher that is the only way to get better, faster. To push you into a mental paradigm of light speed competitive advantages for whatever organization your work for all the while providing better, faster, more comprehensive offerings to your clients and end users. We owe this to them, IT industry has taken on the stench of government cost and time overruns while not even delivering the basics that were agreed upon initially. We, You have to change this perspective, through knowledgeable, comprehensive, accurate systems, applications and offerings that will force the landscape to change. Incumbents no longer get a free pass; never again accept "This is the way things are done". Break through that and other stagnant mindsets by proving them wrong by the results you deliver. Facts are facts and results once delivered cannot be

disproved. That is my aim for all who take on the challenge to not only read but implement the methodologies herein. And launch your career, organization and our industry forward faster!

HOW TO USE:

Even though this book is one in a series, there is no prescribed way to read this book, some concepts and strategies you may already know but would like reassurance or reinforcement, if so fine if not skip it.
Other concepts might be a little foreign to you that's ok, read over it get what you can and research it further if necessary. This is not a "Deep Dive" text. These are strictly proven methodologies to help get the momentum needed in whatever area you deem necessary. I wrote this with the sole purpose that anyone new to IT leadership can pick this up employ the strategies herein and be very productive as a leader. Or the seasoned IT leader can browse through to get some strategies that they may have been unaware of, begin to implement them and adjust course in a stagnant organization. From start-up to fortune 500, these methods work and will continue to work. The more you use them faster you will get the results you are looking for and the more proficient you get with your implementation of

them the better results you will see across the board. The rate of change in IT is blistering and the things that worked yesterday might not work today, it is only getting faster. Whatever your situation, Non-IT business owner, startup founder, fortune 500 executive or entry level employee. The strategies between these pages (Be they physical or digital) will help you get more and continue to get more.

Whenever there is a question as to what your vision or goal is you can fall back to #MORE, to encompass META LEADERSHIP!

BEFORE YOU BEGIN:

Just a word of caution before you begin, this book was written by a professional for professionals, some technical terms are used and I have tried to add very concise descriptions of each. If at any point a term is unfamiliar, please take the time to look it up so that you are up to speed as you continue through the section.

This is not for the easily offended, at times we all get stuck in our ways and think we are on the right path doing the right things only to get to the end and realize that we could have gotten there faster and with much less headache. If you do not take criticism well PUT THE BOOK DOWN NOW. If you are unwilling or scared to implement the strategies PUT THE BOOK DOWN NOW. If you are the type of person that takes processes and or methodologies and personalizes them to the point that when shown wrong or inefficient you get defensive PUT THE BOOK DOWN NOW. If you are scared of tension or putting forth effort in doing the research to get your position across to higher ups PUT THIS BOOK DOWN NOW. If you are scared to be a true leader by protecting your people and buffering them from the non-essential so that they can accomplish the mandatory PUT THE BOOK DOWN NOW. If you are the type of ass that is all about the politics and want leadership positions for the title and the $ only PUT THE BOOK DOWN. If you shun from personal and professional responsibility as well as accountability PUT THE BOOK DOWN, if you can't take your face off of your phone or smart watch during a meeting or conversation PUT THE BOOK DOWN.

Realize now, that people (33%) build devices, systems and applications (33%) for people (33%) (Predominately) and you as a leader have to be on the 66% side of that equation to be even remotely effective. This book is for the committed LEADER, the one who understands that with a great staff comes long hours, weekend and holiday work. One that understands offering constant accessibility to your staff and issue resolution is your primary job. "If my people are working than I am available, if there is an issue I will resolve or devise a plan with those in the know to get it done". One who takes the stance that hiring the right people and giving them guidance and support is the only way forward. Not telling them how to do their jobs, but instead offering coaching and mentor ship. One that understands knowledge work is more taxing than physical. One that understands whether you team/staff is great or awful is in direct correlation to whether the leader is great or awful, THERE ARE NO EXCEPTIONS! Leader sets the culture, culture controls the people, and people do the work. It all starts with you!

General George S. Patton said it best:
"Don't tell people how to do things, tell them what to do and let them surprise you"

Technology touches every industry and in a nightmarish paradox it changes at a faster rate than any other industry. You must accept that; you have to adapt with the changes or get left behind like so many once great organizations and the individuals that not only ran them into the ground but the "yes" men and women that were employed by them that allowed it to happen. Today's IT as well as business leaders have to account for digital disruption at rapidly approaching paranoia levels. No entity, organization or government is beyond its reach. Not manufacturing, financial services, healthcare, retail, construction, legal, transportation, military or even civil infrastructure.

Golden goose projects no longer have years; success is measured in months. They have become what I call "Unicorn's", The ridiculous waste of far too many resources, to develop, implement, integrate or launch a system, service, application or product at the behest of leadership that is disconnected with not only the end user but their staff as well. High paid consultants are brought in with experience and their strategies/processes that worked 5 years ago only to fail massively. Their plans are not the problem and neither are the personnel. The issues can all be traced back to three critical foundations: 1) the information is dated, obsolete or just plain wrong. 2) The level of effort required and or put in is severely lacking. 3) The execution is not happening as planned for unaccounted for reasons. (For a great perspective on levels of effort see: The 10X rule by Grant Cardone). These reasons can be personal, political or financial (see "The Agency Problem") The industry standard development and project management methodologies and "best practices" that try to keep up also go through constant changes, updates, revisions and adaptations: SDLC, Waterfall, RAD, SCRUM, AGILE, Critical Path Method (CPM), Critical Chain Project Management (CCPM) and the list carries on. Project management frameworks such as those pushed by Six Sigma, PMP and PRINCE2 certifications even though highly touted are flawed. Statistics show that overall; IT projects have a failure rate that would get a U.S. high school student expelled. According to a ZDNet study only 42% of IT projects are successful! To put it in perspective that is roughly the attrition rate of the U.S. Army Special Forces indoctrination training!!! A study of 5,400 large scale IT projects (projects with initial budgets greater than $15M) finds that the well-known problems with IT Project Management are persisting. Among the key findings quoted from the report:

- 17 percent of large IT projects go so badly that they can threaten the very existence of the company.
- On average, large IT projects run 45 percent over budget and 7 percent over time, while delivering 56 percent less value than predicted.

(McKinsey & Company in conjunction with the University of Oxford: 2012 Study on large scale IT Projects). Some schools of thought believe that the issue is project complexity: (Speaking ahead of the upcoming Gartner Application Architecture, Development & Integration Summit in Sydney, Darryl Carlton, research director at Gartner, explained that despite the best advice available, information systems are not being built with the same degree of reliability, integrity and predictability as other engineering disciplines. http://www.gartner.com/smarterwithgartner/it-projects-need-less-complexity-not-more-governance/). I disagree; other disciplines have dealt with complexity issues for decades prior to the existence of IT as we know it. You cannot become entrenched anymore to once tried and true methods, you have to hire, grow and trust the right people anything less is business, career or project suicide.

This book was written for mature adult's/IT professionals that want to improve their sphere of influence and that are only beholden to the "Best Way" those that are flexible and understand that the best way today might be obsolete in 6 months. Those that want to move their organizations, clients, teams and peers forward with reduced wasted efforts, reduced frustrations, faster deliveries and higher levels of quality than the present allows as well as higher levels of job satisfaction at higher income levels.

#MORE

"If you have to tell people you are in charge, you really aren't"

IMPORTANT NOTE:
A successful foundation to every endeavor is 1) Adequate Information/Data 2) Level of effort required. And 3) Relentless execution of the plan with follow-up.

*******EXTREMELY IMPORTANT********

If while reading this book you continue to think of an individual currently in your organization or network that fits these traits or has put some of these practices in place, STOP READING NOW and contact them. Align your efforts with them. Some ego's struggle with help, others get downright jealous. You are better and want better for yourself and those that work for you. Tap into their knowledge and expertise, hire them if possible and get out of their way. One key facet of a META LEADER is to know one when you see one. When you see one, support them, at times their pursuits may seem unorthodox and more often than not downright unrealistic. Is it realistic to think wrapping people in a big metal tube and slinging them through the air is sound? No, but aircraft flights happen all day every day. The list of ubiquitous things now that were once so far-fetched could occupy an encyclopedia on its own. As long as its legal and in line with the overall goal of organizational growth, support and champion them the way you would want to be supported when you become one. IT IS GUARANTEED TO PAYOFF, META leaders will do what is necessary to succeed and give you the privilege of paying them instead of your competitors. If you are smart you will learn from them and get an education like no other in the process.

I chose to take a 3 pronged approach as per this section title for a few reasons. Initially I think it's easier to digest when limited to 3 options, this inadvertently is backed by science. Let me tangent for a minute:

Basically psychology studies (see Iyengar et al.) have shown that given only 2 choices the person feels the options are inadequate and think negatively about one or the other. It's the Good/Bad scenario. In pricing strategies this method is used to offer the customer 3 options, which statistics show that they are most likely to choose the middle option as it somehow conveys a safe bet, not the cheapest but not the most expensive; not the lowest quality but not the highest quality either. Any more than three options provides the person with potentially too much information and is off-putting (statistically).

What's the takeaway? More choices might capture consumers' attention, but sheer variety is actually harmful in converting them to customers.

"We might enjoy gazing at those giant walls of mayonnaises, mustards, vinegars, and jams, but we can't do the math of comparing and contrasting and actually picking from that stunning display," Iyengar said.

That's great and all for sales and marketing as well as the studies that get validated by the numbers but that's not why I did it. Thinking logically as engineers tend to do out of habit, I decided to use the method of 3's because a triangle is the only closed shape with the least number of sides. Closed shape is a visual for complete encapsulation of a concept. For arguments sake let's just say that a circle has sides and that at a minimum there are 360 of them.

Moving on........

The method of 3 should be employed by you as a leader as well in a myriad of capacities that you are breaking down a goal, concept or instruction block to your staff. In the military we became quite familiar with this methodology in the form of how directives were given to us based on the following: (Ask anyone that has served about "Task, Conditions and Standards")
1) Task to be done.
2) Conditions under which it will take place. (Resources, Tools, Etc.)
3) Standards that should be adhered to.

It's a dynamic as well as concise format to use ensuring everything needed gets addressed. It's comprehensive enough for control freaks and easy enough for lowest common denominator

mentalities. So that is where I learned the true power of the methodology of 3.
It can be and has been applied to numerous other practices and fields of study.

Examples:
1) People, Processes and Product or Service as a focal point in business.
2) Project Management has Quality, Time and Cost Venn diagram.
3) IT has the Hardware, Network, Application methodology for troubleshooting.
4) Football has Offense, Defense and Special Teams.
5) Atoms are made up of three particles: protons, neutrons and electrons.
And on and on and on, you get the point...

So because you are already familiar with it I tried to remain consistent and allow for the ease of material digestion when it is presented here.
****Did you catch that? Thc method of 3's was one of the foundations of META Leadership. The others will not be delivered in such a hidden manner, so have no fear everything from here on in is straight to the point. Abrasively so in some instances.

The breakdown of the book is as follows:
1) Internal: This is everything relating to your organization staff and resources.

2) External: This is comprised of everything not internally related.
3) Self: This is about you as a person and a leader.

But as far as this writing is concerned I chunk the sections into 1) Context: To provide you a little perspective.
2) How to: To illustrate how to implement the strategy and 3) Results: the potential benefits garnered for this implementation.

Understand there are some over-runs, blurred lines or dependencies between and amongst the 3 but I put them where they have the biggest impact or are most critical, feel free to assemble them how you wish and in a manner that works best for you as the guiding intent of the book is #MORE. However, you work it as long as you achieve more than it is worth it.

CURRENT STATE

INTERNAL

Internally is where you must put forth the most effort to shine externally to your clients/customers. So let's get started.

CONTEXT:

"Show me your processes and I'll show you your problems"

Know your processes and know your numbers, the criticality cannot be overstated. This has stood the test of time everywhere I have ever gone or heard about through the proverbial grapevine. Many, many organizations are more worried about the superficial than the substantial and all it takes is a bump in the road to point out every last one of their deficiencies in the face of failure. Common thought and sadly enough standard operating procedure is to run around being too busy, too busy to document, too busy for due-diligence and on and on.

Understand this one IRON-CLAD FACT: Busy has never meant productive, resourceful or effective. Busy just means occupied with any given task. That does not elevate the task to priority or importance and most often when someone says they are busy it is something they are doing to fill time and escape from doing something of considerably more importance. When I hear people say they are too busy or so busy, all I think is that they are poor time managers and why in the hell are you bragging about it to me.

Look I get it, there is a lot to be done and addressed when you are a leader, which is the standard. But when your people are too busy to follow processes, that is your fault. When your people are operating without processes that is your fault for not ensuring they have them.
Most in IT are under the impression that IT is different than anything else when in fact it's no different than manufacturing. The only difference is the scalability, tangibility and speed. By all accounts whether documented or not there is a process that in most cases haphazardly happens. Whether it's getting network connectivity, setting up servers or VM's, down to development and deployment of an application or platform.

There are user requirements, security concerns, maintenance issues and the like encompassing the entire environment. So yes I said it, we are no different. When developing your process with your staff not for them, ensure that certain criteria is adhered to for example:

All Process should meet the following criteria.
1) They should be repeatable.
2) They should be definable.
3) They should be optimized.
* 4) They should be reviewed at a scheduled frequency dependent on the impact and nature of

the state of the technological domain and/or the rate at which regulatory change occurs.

Remember the goal of process optimization can be boiled down to one word; REDUCTION. Reduction of complexity, technical debt, latency and errors, that is all. Latency being defined as time from start to finish. Complexity and Errors are self-explanatory. Keep your feelings out of the equation, especially if you were the creator of the process. Remain objective and pragmatic throughout the process. From the day you take over as a leader you have to identify, catalog and evaluate every process that happens under your watch, here is where you will get the greatest impact from your efforts. What are the single points of failure that need to be addressed? How are they being addressed currently? Why or why not? Optimization will be addressed later, the focus here is to identify and document any and all processes involved in the end to end functionality of your organization. One framework I have used to ensure conciseness of the documentation as well as identifying any shortcomings is H.A.N.D.S.360®.

Hardware, Applications, Network, Data and Security. The 360 is used as a baseline to identify 360 variables, options, paths, configurations or vulnerabilities across the 5 spectrums. You really have to be careful with this framework however, this can expose a lot of things that you were not trying to find out regarding deficiencies or opportunities and can send you down a never ending rabbit hole Alice! If you want to know more about H.A.N.D.S.360®. Contact me and I will be glad to provide you more information, my contact information is provided at the end of the book.

Is your data ecosystem in order, do you have a MDM (Master Data Management) program, why or why not? If so is it under control, is the movement of every piece of data flowing through your organization mapped, tracked and stored? Moving into the next few decades data will be of critical importance to the growth and sustainability of any and every organization.

HOW TO:

Step one: Mock transaction or War-game installations.

Be the buyer, go through the buying process from end to end, document every step that everyone involved had to take to make the transaction possible. Internal IT departments, Go through the troubleshooting process from call origination to ticket closure. Software development, go through the entire process asking as many questions as possible throughout so that you know what is happening and who is responsible for what step of the process. Be the business owner and conduct an installation or conversion off site just as you would a client.

BREAK THINGS. That's right break things. What if this part doesn't work, what if this system is down, what if this person is out, what if the weather is bad, and what if banks are closed, what if, what if, what if.

If you don't have transactions in the typical sense, step out on the floor, have each position on your staff walk you through their responsibilities and what it is they do to make your organization successful. When coming at them this way you foster a "Positive energy" and thus make it easier to engage.

Tools and methods for process analysis may vary.

***Have each position develop (And ensure they have the time to develop) a RUN BOOK. This should be mandatory within all KNOWLEDGE Workforces. Because you never know when someone is going to be out, or leave your organization. Detailed RUN BOOK's provide you and your staff the ability to continue on with minimal interruption or disruption if the one responsible has in front of them the daily focal points and steps to accomplish.

The analysis tool examples provided are just that only examples, if there is a method you prefer than by all means use that. There are some very light and quick ones like I provided and there are some very deep and involved ones at your disposal like the KANO MODEL, Balanced Scorecard and one that works particularly well is the 7S model as seen below:

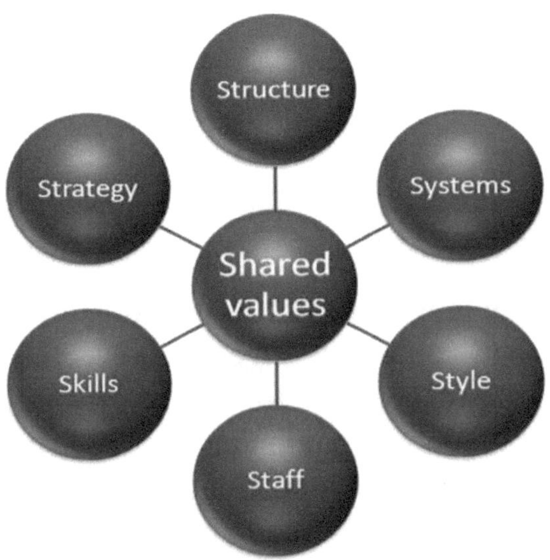

The shape of the "model" was also of monumental importance. It suggested that all seven forces needed to somehow be aligned if the organization was going to move forward vigorously—this was the "breakthrough" (a word I normally despise) that directly addressed Ron Daniel's initial concerns that had motivated the project.

(As per Tom Peters)

Regardless of the methodology you use or the framework you deploy just be sure it captures all aspects of the target for analysis you need in order to adequately and accurately assess the asset in question. This will allow for "Distributed improvements" across the board making everyone and everything more effective and productive in the end, even you.

RESULTS:

These mock transactions for documentation do more than you know. It gets you involved in what you are responsible for. It shows your people that not only are you paying attention but that you want then to be put in a position to succeed and continue to convey that message by eliciting their advice or opinions. They know more than you think because they are the ones right there in the mix, performing the tasks to make that transaction happen. It allows you to justify the reasons for application licenses needed, as well as any subsequent software or system purchases required to get better. Ensuring they have the right tools to do the best job the best way thus getting #MORE out of them.

When done right this will also provide you an inventory of your inputs. To be cataloged in a CMDB (Configuration Management Database),

Application portfolio, Network and or Hardware map, etc.

OF CRITICAL IMPORTANCE*

Do not tell them how to do it, ask questions like why is it done like this or why is it not done like that. Ask them for improvement ideas and take notes. Be diligent and follow up with them if you do take their advice and allow them to implement or remove a step. Have them involved and give them ownership of it as well as get them any quality control issues feedback immediately? You now have documented process for product or service standardization whether it be a flow chart with each step broken down into a checklist, or some other way of disseminating this information to the responsible party.

Optimization, now with a process in hand you can review it to try and remove redundancies or wasted steps thus making that part of the process cheaper and in effcct more efficient.

If you only take one thing from the book take this and exercise it liberally with every part of your organization. If you focus on only one thing ensure that it is your processes, this will allow your insight into more aspects of your business than any other area even accounting and it is the only way to identify ephemeral costs that miss the balance sheets but still eat away at your budget like "MEETINGS" uuuggghhh!

PERSONAL NOTE:

If you claim to not have the time to document and formalize your staffs' processes and review them for opportunities/deficiencies or have no inclination to involve yourself at their level guiding them not telling them how, take your sorry ass home because you are not a META Leader. You are nothing more than a "PAPER CHAMPION" and going to cost shareholders, business owners, employees not only money but potentially their jobs and do more damage than good the longer you continue to steal your salary. If you got offended by this, then you are exactly who I am talking to and about.

CONTEXT:

"Your people ARE your organization"

Everyone knows someone who works for an organization they despise, why is that? It could be the individual just has an overall bad attitude or it could be the leadership of that organization is similar to many others that management does not realize the actual capacity of their job. By that I mean MANAGING people. As I stated in the previous section “People build systems/application for people”. Not discounting the importance of any other of the job functions of leadership but the ones who are staffed with a despondent workforce are Captaining the titanic and that ice berg is not that far off. What are your processes or policies for succession planning? Do your people know what their “next level” is for your organization? Do you keep a staff profile that is easily accessible for you in times of meetings or if they request to meet with you? What is your office communication plan, is it flat or a hierarchy? Why or why not? What are the single points of failure that need to be addressed from a staff perspective? How are they being addressed currently?

HOW TO:

Step one: Review files to get a snapshot of core competencies. The resumes and credentials of those whom you are in charge of should be read by you and if possible put into some sort of digital capabilities repository. This will ultimately give you a high level view of the overall core competencies of your staff. Then similar to the steps in Processes, take a trip or invite them in and talk to them gauge their interests, what they like or do not like about the organization (TAKE NOTES). Ask their opinions regarding certain policies. Find out their goals and see how they align or if you can align them with those of your organization.

Get to know your people, once you know your peoples' strengths and weaknesses you are much better equipped to position them at the right place with the right tools to successfully accomplish the assignments to which they are tasked.

I was watching an episode of 30 Rock where Jack was being shown flash cards of those that worked under him. He would have to accurately name the person on the card. Your team/staff or organization may not be that big but the point that gets highlighted is one in which when you can call someone by their name it reinforces a rapport. Also when speaking to them initially try to figure out their eye color, not that this has any bearing from an information stance but when you look someone in the eyes as they are speaking it lets them know that you are "In the moment" and that you are actually paying attention.

There is a technique called S.O.F.T.E.N. use this and use it liberally to continue building rapport with not only your staff but those that you report to as well. This technique can be applied on almost every occasion of engagement with anyone.

The breakdown is as follows:

Smile, Open posture, Forward lean, Take notes, Eye contact, Nodding.

Employ it not only at work but socially to get practice and the most out of it you possibly can. It works and it works well. There are volumes already available regarding body languages role in effective communication so I will not go into a litany of them here just know that it is science has been documented comprehensively.

Tools For Analysis:

1) Core Competence Analysis:

Employee ID	Name	Hardware	Network	Date
1	Joe Smith	4	5	
2	Mike Jones	2	9	
3	Tim James	1	7	

In the above example we can see whose strengths are in what key area. I specifically like this matrix because it can be easily loaded into a database and the more data gets added the more robust it becomes and you can see where your staffing strengths really are and better align them to positions within the organization. Remember this is just a base template; you can create your own with more specific fields for a better drill down analysis of who has what capabilities within each specific unit or department.

RESULTS:

The results of this are twofold, initially it is the overall assessment of the staff you have, their core-competencies their interest and motivations as well as a manner and means of rapport building. To garner trust and gain the respect of your people is paramount for any leader but especially to that of a META Leader.

OF CRITICAL IMPORTANCE*

Be extremely aware of certain company policies that may be in violation and do not cross them with regards to certain topics discussed, times that you meet or socialize with members of your team/staff. There could be considerable company/career/legal implications if you are not careful.

PERSONAL NOTE:

It is much better to be respected than loved. However, there is nothing that prevents respect and likability. Remember this is not the stage for you to impress upon them your ideas; it is only for you to assess the state and culture of what you are working with.

CONTEXT:

"We see our customer as invited guests to a party, and we are the hosts. It's our job every day to make every important aspect of the customer experience a little bit better"
Jeff Bezos, CEO Amazon

If you don't know what you produce and how it affects the lives and businesses of your customers your time in a leadership position should be "SHORT LIVED". You should know your service extremely well, you should know what features are being added and or removed so that you can be proactive in updating or alerting clients of any negative impacts from a damage controls perspective. I read once that every product in your home is nothing more than a trophy! It is a victory for one company/producer/provider over all others. If you really think about it, this is correct. Their marketing won, their distribution won, their branding and advertising won.

I remember a trip I was on and ran into a medical device manufacturer's CIO on a plane. He struck up a conversation with me as our flight sat out on the tarmac awaiting clearance for takeoff. I was speaking to him about what is it really like being the CIO of a considerably large organization likes dislikes etc. Completely implementing the S.O.F.T.E.N. technique mentioned earlier. This gentleman was fairly intelligent and put together in his demeanor and delivery. I asked him about the devices and his answer was, "Something to do with dialysis or kidneys, I really couldn't tell you that much about them as I have only been there a year"! This accomplished leader who told me he was directly responsible for the software of a medical device that augments kidney functions for presumably hundreds of thousands of human beings doesn't really know. I was shocked, not that I expected him to quote lines of code or speak about API's for data collection and monitoring or any deeply technical constructs. But DAMN, talk about disconnected. I leaned back in my seat as the pilot announced that we had take-off approval, and thanked him for his time all the while wondering how that could happen.

The complete separation of management from his products blew me away. Why was he not excited to tell me about advances his people are making, or how they have the best data accuracy, or the most sensors for the most comprehensive monitoring and reporting of chemical levels etc. Even excited about the average level of education being a PhD for his entire staff, something, anything. This was a lesson for me and obviously it stuck, I will never be in the position in which I am so far removed from whatever my offering is that I cannot tell anyone extensively about it. That is a ship without a captain as far as I am concerned.

HOW TO:

Step one: Experience the use of your organizations services. Start from the beginning, log in, log on, try to connect, make changes, personalize, send an email, connect a monitor, print a document, complete a transaction. Whatever it is "LIVE the customer experience" from the products or services you provide. Take notes, ask questions, call help desk, call current customers ask them what they like and dislike. Become intimately involved with every feature, benefit, defect, deficiency or bug your products and/or services have to offer. Document and take notes continuously about everything and every aspect.

Be a secret shopper, conduct open audits, and ask staff their likes, dislikes, ideas and solutions. Be as diligent as possible when learning about the Talking points as well as the subtle nuances of what you are charging the customer for. Build up your knowledgebase so that you can speak about your services with the depth of a dedicated salesman.

Tools for Analysis:

2) Core Competence Analysis for an application or service:

Service ID	Name	Response Time	Ease of use	Date
1	App 1	5	5	
2	App 2	9	2	
3	App 3	7	7	

In the above example we can see what the feature stack of the system or application looks like. Similar to the preceding section this format can be easily loaded into a database and the more data gets added the more robust it becomes and you can see where your product/service feature strengths really are and better align them to what the users are asking for as well as conduct baselines against competitors' products/services.

RESULTS:

You are forever a salesman, anytime you are asked what you do, there is a reason for you to be knowledgeable, anytime your kids tell about your job to their friends or their friends parents there is a reason to brag about your services, people and organization. I heard a saying once that "you should never tell people your problems, because

50% don't care and the other 50% are glad you have them". I have never been in a situation that excitement wasn't contagious even for a little bit. If you know about what you do and you are excited about it you will have confidence, confidence that you don't have to say it will project off of you like a beam of light. Your people will be able to speak to you about issues without having to dumb things down; they will overwhelmingly get the sense that you are paying attention to them and their efforts. You will be able to adequately and accurately address any of your customers with the knowledge, answers and feedback they expect leadership to have.

OF CRITICAL IMPORTANCE*

Do as much reading and documenting about your offerings as you possibly can if you are new, at times it may feel as though you are drinking from a fire hose. Don't worry it will pay dividends later on. If possible never turn down an opportunity to be in on a code review or a release management meeting even an on-site installation at random times will add much to you and what you know.

PERSONAL NOTE:

The more you know about your product the more knowledgeable you will be, the more accurately you will speak and thus the more respect you will have that is deserved.

EXTERNAL

Externally is where you need to focus next in an effort to assess the environment, in which you will be operating,

CONTEXT:

"Defined processes lead to superior decisions"

I wanted to reinforce the importance of the value of time and decision making, how processes can lead to almost "Oracle/Sage" level insight regarding next course of actions to take as a leader. In keeping with the power of 3's I have broken this section down a little further into the following: 1) Clients, 2) Vendors, 3) Partners and the processes you have in place for those interactions. All of this is leading you to gather the information you need to be in complete control of the situations for which decisions have to be made.

I once heard a story regarding the excellence of University of Alabama head football coach Nick Saban. The story goes as follows (a paraphrase of course). He tries to focus on decisions. That's all, He spends his seconds and minutes of each practice, play and game focused on making the best decisions he can at that moment. His math for this is pretty sound. Stated "No one makes 100% best decisions all of the time, but if I can make 8-9 great decisions out of 10 I know I will be successful". Not bad at all, 80%-90% success rate is astonishing in today's hyper competitive industries be they athletics, academics, industry, politics or parenting. Understand this in no way guarantees success but it increases your odds substantially.

So how do you know if you are making the right decisions, prior to experimenting and trial and error scenarios? What are your processes? What are their success rates? Did you follow them or did you wing it? Were you distracted? Take the time at the end of the day to evaluate the decisions you made that day.

If you are honest you will realize that you have room for tremendous improvement. Do you interact with clients, vendors or partners with an agenda, what is the purpose for that specific engagement or encounter, how does it benefit your organization, did you accomplish your intentions, why or why not?

Time is the most valuable asset any human being has; paramount to respect is respect for the time of others. Referencing back to the previous section regarding "busy". I will restate I loathe that term/word. Time wasters are busy, Organizational management by means of firefighting is just another sign that the person conducting such is not skilled enough for the position they have been given. I am in complete agreement with the cliché "Lack of planning on your part does not necessitate an emergency on mine". So rule number one for all of your external processes:

Ensure they are efficient and effective, always, always, always account for the respect of others time. This is where process latency comes into place. Once again: Latency being defined as time from start to finish. How long do your transactions take? How long are your sales meetings? How long are your candidate interviews? Understand I am not talking about rushing things and exposing yourself or organization to errors, But rather careful consideration has to be exercised and all critical details covered but in a manner that expedites the process and not monopolizing the life of this individual.

PART I CLIENTS:

Do you conduct A/B testing (not just on marketing but the usability/functionality aspects of your offerings also), if not how did you decide on that ad, application path UI/UX, etc. Was the most effective, fastest or accurate at achieving your aims from a customer/end user perspective?
There is a direct correlation between the number of conversations you are having versus the sales you are closing. What is working, what has a higher hit/closing rate and what does not? Do you ask your current and past clients for referrals and testimonials, why or why not? Do you go out and visit the clients, watch them use your products and/or services. Actual users watching their actions and interactions. Maybe they found a use

for your service that you were unaware of (The use of baking soda for odor control in the refrigerator as an example). The tale goes as follows: Arm & Hammer had no idea that women were using their product for odor control until they conducted a few home visits for market research. Upon inquisition one of the researchers stumbled across the product sitting in the back of a refrigerator at one of their customers' homes. When he asked why she kept it in there she told him why and there you have it, brand new use for the product without massive cost of R&D. Your end users are your best method for feedback, product line extension and innovation, find out what they used elsewhere (intro into Competitive Intelligence), what they liked and didn't like about it, what makes that provider/vendor better or worse than you. Document all of that, it is basically inverse consulting (Companies paying you to tell you what they want to buy). How did you decide to add that feature that cost X to develop or implement? Do you take time to find out you client KPI's and see if there is a way for you to provide an offering to assist them with those? Do you provide your clients with a breaking set?
Do you work with clients on journey lines, helping them through the use of your products or services to optimize some of their own internal processes? Have you tried transaction leveraging with your clients (Similar to a bank charging a fee for a loan application as well as interest on the loan, 2

sources of income on a single transaction.) If so, how is that working, if not, why not and is it documented. What are your processes for contract rejections, follow ups and who is responsible?

What is our process for generating value for our clients, specifically? What about the data generated by your users? Is it mapped, tracked and stored at a minimum? Is it being analyzed and if so by whom, using what tools and/or applications? Feedback data, complaint data, testimonials and usage data. All of these need to be documented and you will see why later on. Data strategies when implemented correctly can open vast amounts of never expected income opportunities for a lot of organizations and huge bonuses for you.

PART II VENDORS:

Your vendors are everyone you pay money to that are not on your payroll, period. This includes technology providers, staffing firms, outside consultants etc. Practice your interviews and engagements for as many situations you can that you encounter most throughout your day, week or month. This will give you a feel for how much time you are wasting or in effect STEALING from yourself and the others involved. Think about it terms of money, calculate the cost of the time for all involved and then ask yourself if that is a cost you would pay if it was coming out of your own pocket. That one practice will get you in the habit of concise but still comprehensive encounters. Once you do this and become proficient at it, tell people that you are doing it and tell them why. Let them know that not only is their time important to you but so is yours. You will start to see the respect and effective nature of interactions come back to you in return because you will start to get a reputation as a true professional.

From the day you decide you need to fill a position until the day they are proficient enough to manage their own day? What is our on-boarding process like for both client and employee? Go through it yourself, mock interview, staffing companies, paperwork, tax, background check, drug screening etc. What is discouraging to potential candidates, what was discouraging or encouraging to you? Are you and your process keeping up with current trends or not. Maybe this is the reason you are not getting the talented candidates you think you should. While we are on the subject of "Staffing firms", it is critical that you audit them as well. My experience with them has been depressing on average. I have had one great recruiter in my entire career and the rest were a bunch of used car salesmen and women.

My experience has been on both ends from candidate to client and the overwhelming majority are, in my opinion useless on their best days. Their drive to get the most money they can from an organization while paying as little as possible to the candidate, this is a recipe for lasting problems. They will never have you or your candidates' best interests at the forefront. Understand I am not down on the entire industry, there are those that go above and beyond and that do deserve their premiums, but most shops are not worth the price they paid to acquire their business license. Mystery shop them, set up fake candidates with fake interviews, see how much they are taking from the candidates because this will definitely have an impact on the quality of the candidates that make it to your doorstep.

Do you locate other opportunities and find out what it takes to become a vendor? Do you have process in place for vetting those who want to come on as a vendor to your organization? Why or why not? Who is responsible, what is the average timeline, what is redundant or discouraging? Go through the process identify what works and what does not. What about government contracting? Are you eligible, if so establish this even if you do not want to provide services to the government, some of your clients probably are and would like to know that they are in compliance regarding 3rd party providers. What are your policies for vendor management? This can be critical in the event they provide a mandatory asset and are unable to fulfill their contract obligations, what happens then? Who is responsible for managing that situation?

PART III PARTNERS AND OTHERS:

Take time to speak with your partners. Microsoft, Oracle, Cisco, Amazon AWS, Google Apps for business etc. Whoever you have partnerships with, take the time to speak and meet with them. If they provide content ask them what works and what does not, discuss conversion rates or interest generation, feedback they have received etc. Know which of their services work, which ones don't. Leverage those relationships as much as possible, they can pay off tremendously and they have dedicated resources that your organization is in no way willing to commit so use it. Visit with strangers and ask them for thoughts about your marketing materials, thoughts on the website? Are your demos to long, to short, not enough information, too much information (Remember to respect others time!). Get friends to mystery shop, call or visit the office, ask others around your building what are their thoughts about your company and its people, maybe you have a PR disaster brewing that would have otherwise gone undetected. What are your processes for damage control from a branding perspective? On Marketing and Branding do you exercise Newsjacking, why or why not? Sounds awful but it is actually pretty fantastic, if you believe in your offerings. Newsjacking happens all of the time, a storm hits an area and a major insurance carrier has teams on site giving out water and blankets or

Tide sends mobile washing units to provide laundry services to the citizens in the hardest hit areas. All while inviting the national media to speak with their representatives and show their services in action. Free national commercial advertisement.

**Regulatory and Compliance:
This is up to your legal department if you are in a regulated sector but ask about meeting with and discussing key issues with those regulatory authorities. However, regarding these encounters and engagements one must ensure that there are no legal implications surrounding this.

HOW TO:

Step one: In your next meeting, compare the events of such with what you just read and note anywhere there are deficiencies or where it complies with respecting others time.

Great you have a meeting with a client, whether they are voicing a complaint or want to buy more of your product or services its irrelevant. When the organizer sets up the meeting review what occurs against a checklist. Your agenda checklist can go as follows:

- Start Date and Time: (Always start on time, no matter what)
- Thank everyone for their time.
- Purpose:
- Attendee list and why each individuals presence has been requested:
- Specific Issues/Opportunities to be resolved:
- (As each one gets resolved check them off and never go back)
- Actions Items(if necessary) as well as who is responsible for them and a completion timeline:
- Closing Remarks/Comments/Notices:
- Stop time: (Always end on time)
- Thank attendees for their time. (Yes, again. Everyone likes to know you think they are important)

The above is just an example and can be tailored to fit your specific needs based on any given encounter. But the benefits are far reaching; does everyone know when they need to be there, why they are there, what they need to do, by when and when they will be free. Did the organizer take advantage of those individuals time because he/she was in a position of authority, these are questions you need to continually ask when auditing and engaging.

The reason I chose the example I did for step one is based on getting you to realize and put into practice the value of time. A truck load of other options are given in the context section. As you are becoming aware of by this point in your reading take advantage of as many as you can, as much as you can. This will continue to solidify your position as a truly professional knowledge worker and grow your options when making decisions thus enhancing the decisions that you ultimately make.

RESULTS:

The benefits are unimaginable. Use all of this information to enhance your credibility as well as your organizational intelligence. This ultimately plays into the making of supremely better decisions based on your external facing processes. At this point you can start using Functions of probability with your decisions. You will gather more insight into the actual operations of an organization than anyone else is willing to and set you head and shoulders above your peers with your insight into deficiencies and opportunities of the organization with which you are employed. Thus affording you even more time to continue to evaluate the decisions you are making and hence make better decisions faster increasing your overall effectiveness as a leader and more importantly a person. It becomes a monster that feeds on itself or a "Flywheel" as so eloquently described in detail by one Jim Collins in his book "Good to Great". And you better believe others will stand in awe at how you do what you do with the ease they dream of.

OF CRITICAL IMPORTANCE*
People's time is of critical importance, this is common sense but in no organization that I have ever been a part of has this been common practice. When you start finding more time, do not find the need to fill it with senseless tasks or for catching up on anything but refining your decision-making skills. Evaluate the outcomes of decisions you have made and if they worked to your liking why or why not. The key component of any META Leader is their ability to make quality decisions with consistency and certainty. Remember you are still in the discovery phase continue to document all processes even those that are nonexistent because those harbor your greatest potential for opportunities and to achieve great strides not just for your career but for the advancement of your organization as well. Understanding that, Have

more conversations with even more people. Get known, known for respect, for professionalism, for attention to details. BE ON THE RADAR!

PERSONAL NOTE:

The respect of a leader that has deep knowledge and insights is most valuable in times of turbulence, when things are good it's easy to be a good leader. It's when things are going from bad to worse, that those individuals who have put in the work and research in identifying, isolating and resolving cascade issues or take rapid advantages of opportunities to turn the situation around. Meta Leaders are able to pull off what others deem as miracles and do so with the up most confidence. This is done by knowing as much as you can about the environment as well as the industry your organization operates in. In military terms this is called Battlesapce awareness. However, for this domain we can refer to it as "BUSINESSSPACE AWARENESS"

CONTEXT:

"You are only as strong as your weakest link"

I hesitate a little on this section because there are potential HR implications and I am not well versed on any of those criteria or constraints. I do however understand the epic importance of that department and the functions they provide.

So here we go………

What are you doing to incentivize your people the right way? The days of 3%-5% annual raises based on performance reviews are a relic of days past. If you are still doing this stop, it's bad for your people and bad for your overall business/department performance. Depending on the culture you have in place try out different kinds of incentives, bonus structures, percentages of total growth based on direct contribution etc. There are numerous concerns other than $ that individuals are looking for these days. Paid time off, College classes, Certification training, So forth and so on. This in the realm of building your people and your organization. What do you have now? What do your people like about it? What are others in your industry doing? Keep up and stay competitive with the marketplace or be faced with the ever-increasing lack of available talent. News flash: THERE IS NO TALENT SHORTAGE IN IT!

<u>SIDE NOTE ON TALENT:</u>

3 Reasons Why the "Talent Shortage Issue" is an inside job! #1. Look internally: Not for the talent (you could do that as well though.) but at your hiring/staffing processes. If your hiring process takes longer than a ONE WEEK you have a problem. YES, the problem being your organization is inefficient and that may just be indicative of bigger organizational issues. #2 (Still inside) I know you are "Busy", so is everyone else, but busy does not mean productive and if you or your staff is too busy to conduct interviews and staff up, then Leadership and planning is the problem. #3 (Still you) Do you even know what you need, doubtful. I have seen so many job descriptions that are basically asking for Linus Torvalds to do what an entry level intern could manage. Fill out a position RUNBOOK and go from there. Finally:**Pay your people according to the problem being solved. After all its YOUR problem. There are exceptions to all of the above I acknowledge, but THERE IS PLENTY OF TALENT AVAILABLE, The problem is organizational, i.e YOURS.

Talk, Talk, Talk to your staff and cultivate a culture of honesty regarding what motivates them. What are they saying about your organization on social Media? This is where the legality concerns come into place. What is and what is not off limits. You can offer challenges though if your staff is willing. Post articles and newsworthy clips promoting your organization and challenge them for likes and or views.

What professional organizations are they involved in, Meet-Up groups, etc. Incentivize them to grow their exposure and include your organizations branding. Be sure to take precaution regarding these steps as you do not want to get caught up in anything that could be potentially damaging your brand. What are your content creation processes and policies or those outside of your marketing department if you have one? What are your processes for tutorial development videos for posting to YouTube etc?

Do you have your staff writing whitepapers, books, conducting off-site training? These are extremely valuable for promoting your organization as well as the growth of your people. Do you tout the accomplishments of your staff on your marketing material and site? Do your clients know how good your people are, how professional and accomplished they are? Do you have a "Meaningful" awards program? Why or why not? Scientific studies have shown the efficacy of unexpected rewards that foster intrinsic motivation and continue motivating to a far better degree than static incentives that placate extrinsic motivation.

Do you encourage them to compete in code competitions, or network challenges? What about being speakers or conducting seminars? Do you sponsor or offer them opportunities to participate in “Hack-a-thons”. These events alone are a gold mine for finding the specific talent you may need for your own organization on top of offering a very effective tool for networking. Your staff can be some of the most influential and effective promoters of your business or organization. Do you encourage them to participate in Alumni groups and local business networking events, activities or charitable organizations? Do you sponsor research trips for key members of your staff allowing them to circulate around the industry actively pursuing opportunities and gathering information that cannot be gleaned from web searches or industry journals? Why or why not? Technology is an investment just like the knowledge workers that make it happen and keep it running. If you fail to realize this and take precautions to keep things humming along, I guarantee you will enter a state of reactionary management. Or in terms we are all familiar with a “Culture of firefighting”, were your staff spends 90% of their time responding to emergencies and “hot” items. That is an epic struggle that takes an accomplished META leader to not only stop but also turn around. So please do not attempt to block and counter the point with "Budgetary constraints" or "We don't have the time" (Refer back to resources wasted on meetings if necessary).

Do you foster a culture of constant learning and keeping up with industry trends? META Leaders mantra: "If there is anything we do, that someone else knows how to do better, I want to know what they know and how they do it". This is an opportunity to build an "Anti-Knowledge Registry". From a strategic perspective an AKR is a repository that allows you and your people to focus on things you do not know that can impact your organization. It is in essence a focused risk registry. Always learning, applying what you know and growing because of it. A truly amazing culture will be noticed by the environment in which you operate. Have you ever been to Disney World? There is a reason they call it Magic Kingdom and the happiest place on earth. I took my girls there one summer and that place was amazing from start to finish. It was unbelievably hot and humid, that didn't matter, it was extremely expensive, and that didn't matter either. The staff and somehow all of the visitors that day were in a great mood. Everyone was smiling and laughing throughout the entire day. Kids were at their peaks with screaming and pure joy; you could see and even feel it. The environment was amazing, the crew dressed in costumes was beyond helpful and all smiles. From the characters to the "cast" member tasked with cleanup. Everyone we encountered was par excellence. That will be a study for another day but that is a culture driven and dripping with better. If you have never been I would definitely advise it, even if only to study, you will enjoy it.

HOW TO:

Step one: Have your staff teach each other classes. This is the first step in building programs that build people.

Implement a new program amongst your staff for each individual to research a new or emerging technology and present its implementation and functionality to your staff. This helps in accomplishing a few things.

1) Forces looking outward
2) Builds research skills
3) Builds presentation skills
4) Builds communication skills
5) Grows your staff's knowledgebase for possible future solutions.

I know you will hear or say things like you don't have time, or they do not have the time. I will counter with do you honestly think your staff works all 8 or however many hours a day straight through? Do you? Those questions are rhetorical. Here is how this really works, not only does this allow for great venues of information dissemination, but when tasked with going out into the local community and teaching students about technology or a partnership at the local college or university for professional development classes delivered by your staff they are prepared and have practiced the fundamentals. Thus enhancing their own skills as well as promoting your organizational agenda.

RESULTS: ________________________________

OF CRITICAL IMPORTANCE*

Build loyalty and a culture of growth amongst your staff and they will work miracles for you. If you have the ego that you need to be the one always making things happen you will never be META and even though you may be able to accomplish something great, I guarantee that it won't be done alone.

CONTEXT:

Ubuntu- “I am what I am because of who we all are”

There is no one solution fits all. This is and will continue to be true across all industries. That being said, Interoperability, integration, implementation, adoption are paramount for whatever technology and/or service you provide. What are the systems that your offerings need to work with? What ERP system do your clients have that your applications need to integrate with? This above and beyond has led to the demise of 2 CIO’s that I personally know of. Applications that operate in a silo are months away from their eminent demise and the provider of such will not be far behind if they do not have a follow on strategy. There are tools and technologies that DOMINATE their marketplace, they are doing that now because they have realized that to isolate your services is paramount to cancer. Whether they released/exposed API’s, SDK’s, platforms or plugins. Ignore this at your peril. The technology community is a community because of leveraged interoperability. We do what we do and we do it well, you do the same and together we offer services that are stronger against disruption. This "co-creation" paradigm is not going away anytime soon. Apple integration MS office for IOS, Facebook and Java SDK's, the Visual Studio IDE working with Python, php and Java. Sales force, Google and the list goes on. If these Juggernauts realized this then you had better accept it and move forward to offer solutions that your clients can meet their needs and are easily adopted into their current networks and systems.

Look around your market, what are the complimentary applications, and systems? Which ones do your services work with? How easy is the integration? IS it mapped? Is it tested and re-tested? What API's can you expose? Are your services portable? Extensible? Scalable? This all matters, it matters for longevity, it matters to your clients (Current and future). What is the capability for clients or end users to manage and or grow your current offerings allowing you unseen opportunities? This is where "Next Practices" take over Best practices. What processes do you have in place to monetize fixes and interoperability solutions you have deployed or running internally?

This could be an enormous source of untapped revenue or a bonus feature for your own offerings portfolio. There are countless system integrators that run into a myriad of issues when trying to get systems to work well together. But if they don't know you have solved this then they do not know to contact your organization in an effort to leverage the fix. Back to the concept of having your people continuously get better, have them write a whitepaper on it or if you can position this solution as a potential entry point for other offerings have them post it to an organizational GitHub account, a partners site in the FAQ section or even stackoverflow.

HOW TO:

Co-Creation: Work with your clients to identify solutions they are using. Find out what they like and do not like about these solutions. See if these issues can be solved by one of your offerings. When you identify any shortcomings, build a solution and contact the other provider offering to connect and collaborate on the merging and adoption of the 2 technologies. This is not 100%, some will want nothing to do with you, but META leaders will recognize the opportunities you are offering by combining forccs on this key functionality and commit the resources required to make it happen.

RESULTS:

OF CRITICAL IMPORTANCE*

Leveraging interoperability partnerships. The context part hopefully impressed this criticality of developing and advancing solutions that easily work with other service provider's solutions.

Now the hard part, look at yourself, you have to assess what you as a person, individual and leader know and more importantly believe. A lot of you may be tempted to skip this part, I would caution against that. No matter your thoughts there are things we know about ourselves that we often hide. Certain deficiencies and or character flaws we may choose to ignore. On the other hand, we have substantial assets that we love to focus on, that's ok also. But this is an important part of the META Leader, to know who and what you are just as well as knowing who and what you are not.

CONTEXT:

"If one does not know to which port one is sailing, no wind is favorable". – Seneca

Do you control your day or are you controlled by it? This is one of the most powerful questions I have ever been asked. It forces ownership back to you. Yes, you are responsible for what you did or did not accomplish that day. The excuses available are as long as Google search results if you want to deflect responsibility. On the other hand, if you are like most, you do have a plan for your day and for some reason it always takes a detour and before you know it the day is winding down and there you sit with a to-do list that is probably the same length as when you wrote it.

Most people think they have a plan for the day and low and behold from the moment their feet hit the ground the world comes at them with distractions and disruptions. We operate at a frenzied pace working through the day putting out fires and impromptu meetings, then lunch then after lunch situations that arise ad infinitum. Now, is any of this productive, is it healthy? A well known statistic is that you are at highest risk of heart attack on Mondays between the hours of 6am and 10am. Why do you think that is? My non-medical opinion is that it is the stress of anticipation the looming cloud carrying nonexistent problems. In the movie "After Earth" Will Smith offers up the greatest quote regarding fear I have heard to date:

"Fear is not real. The only place that fear can exist is in our thoughts of the future. It is a product of our imagination, causing us to fear things that do not at present and may not ever exist. That is near insanity. Do not misunderstand me danger is very real but fear is a choice."

How true is this, how gut punchingly accurate is that simple movie quote? But the sad part being, that is the manner the majority carry out their days only to get to the end and think of how miserable they were living that way. There is no law that says you must live and think like this. There is no dictum I have found within the endless legal jargon for any company policy that states anything as such. It is a learned state of mind and as such it can and has to be unlearned. You have to control your day, you are required to take the reins of your life because it's the only one you have and your potential is not going to wait on you to get it together or figure it out and neither will your staff.

HOW TO:

Look at your day and do an assessment of what your usual schedule is. Write it out and see how dependable it is. List everything that is productive and that which is not. Are you a late sleeper, a slow driver, a work socializer? All of these things consume valuable time that could be applied back to productive task for you and your organization.

Make a to-do list the night before, do not re-write the bible. A lot of the discontent I see regarding these daily lists is when individuals have to-do lists that require a turning of the page. That's fine for a goals list but a to-do list should be no more than 3 items broken down to the smallest task possible. The reason is ultimately because you will never get through a long list without an obsession level of commitment. The reality is that most are not that committed it is only a wish list and thus it gets treated with the importance of such.

As a META Leader you do not have this luxury, your time and mental capacity are extremely valuable and have to be treated as so. Make a list of the top 3 things you must complete for that day. Start small if this is new to you and build up to complex tasks. But do it starting today. Understand that, well maybe there are some things one may objectively be view as non-productive but could actually be very productive. Taking breaks to clear your mind or getting away from the screen for an hour or so might provide you the opportunity to get out and experience something that offers you a viable solution. So its ok to be critical of some things other are a necessity to prevent burn out and silo or isolated thoughts that will never lead to anything productive.

One place you can start if you have never taken a Meyers Briggs personality assessment Test is to try it. It is widespread and there are a lot of sites that allow you to take the test for free. This will provide you some feedback on your personality strengths and weaknesses as well as provide some feedback on possible career choices where your personality type will excel. Take it more than once, I actually recommend taking it at least 5 times with various vendors or sites that way you can get a more accurate assessment on the average.

Assess everything even down to how you conduct meetings or conference calls. What you put in emails and why you send them. Do you answer emails promptly; do you return calls within a respectable amount of time. Do you leave people with actions items, do you inform people why a meeting has been called, do you have an agenda that you adhere to, and do you reiterate and ask if anyone needs any clarity regarding any directives given? Do you ensure all relevant questions have been answered? Or do your meetings turn into conversations? Do your calls turn into chats etc? Seriously analyze what you do and how you do it.

In the end it's about control, it's about the respect for time (Yours as well as others) and if you can't even control your own day how are you expected to be able to control your team, staff or organization. Stop running around putting out fires. Plan better, read more and be ready to implement contingency plans when needed. But at all costs control your day.

RESULTS:

When you start to get a handle on your own personal processes you will immediately feel better. Your stress levels will dramatically reduce and you will be better able to deal with the problems as they arise. You will become more relaxed and a lot more confident in what you have going on and this will definitely be felt by your staff.

OF CRITICAL IMPORTANCE*

Be honest when mapping out your day and be honest when designating things as productive and nonproductive. This will provide you with your own guidelines for personal process improvements. However, you can't improve it if you don't identify it.

PERSONAL NOTE:

I take breaks and I take them often. When I do however, I look for someone to talk to or I am on my phone reading science, technology or business news articles to shift my mental focus and potentially spark an insight that I might not have otherwise came across.

CONTEXT:

"Show me the 3 people you associate and communicate with the most and I will show you your future"

The importance of those you surround yourself with is more important to your future than you can ever imagine. If you are the alpha, find new associates, if you are the smartest, find new associates, if you are the superlative in most categories when it comes to your network, crew, friends or associates complacency is about to kill you. You should always be looking to better yourself and your environment. Never suffer fools, never surround yourself with yes men, never accept a relationship career or personal in which the other person or people do not push you or motivate you to continuously grow and get better.

Those you have in your life should support your growth. In a healthy way, not necessarily in dogged competition (Even though sometimes competition is great at pushing us beyond our perceived limits). You should frequently have conversations about ideas and opportunities, problems and their solutions. This expands your mind as well as humbles you as to not allow the opportunity to think you are the most intelligent. They should provide you with insight and perspective even when it's difficult for you. This will inevitably translate into your leadership style. As it will offer you the capacity to listen and grow at work and with your staff. Always on the table should be conversations about opportunities and progress, plans and ideas for advancement and an ambition that cannot be stifled.

The people around you should be achievers, those that have achieved notable accomplishments. Rising out of poverty, overcoming seemingly insurmountable odds, those with expansive institutional education backgrounds, those with expansive life experiences, those who have tried and failed numerous times but have not been deterred. Men and women that have gone through some of life's greatest challenges and made it. You want these people in your life and in your list of contacts that you can call by their first names. You want them for guidance. You want them to bounce ideas off of. You want them around and to know their stories to prevent you from those pathetic moments of self-pity. Or for those moments when you fail and they can offer advice on why it happened and how to prevent it in the future.

You want them as family, friends and co-workers. You want a staff made up of diverse individuals with diverse backgrounds to aid in faster more creative and accurate problem solving.

HOW TO:

Similar to the preceding two parts of this Methodology of 3 conduct a real assessment of those around you. Of the groups you are a part of, the networks you circle in the organizations you are a part of. Do this as soon as possible and at least once per year. Seriously take stock of those in your life and ask yourself if they are pushing you further, if they are inspiring you, if they challenge you to grow if they facilitate your happiness and success. With a lot of these individuals you may already know the answer and it may be difficult for you to accept. I started the book out with the warning that this was for those willing to take action, willing to do what was necessary to get better, to be better to achieve more. If there are those in your life that do not meet your criteria, then you already know that their removal is necessary. I am not saying call them up and tell them anything negative. I am advocating that you spend less and less time interacting with them. Over time they will get the point, people understand that life does move on and that we fall out of touch with those that we once thought we would have around forever. In this regard time is on your side and absolutely an asset.

On the other hand, you know of those that do meet your criteria, immediately tell them. Let them know you appreciate their candor and guidance. Thank them for always trying to get you to see the big picture, the potential. These are your star players, these are the relationships you need to nurture and strengthen. I have a task list every morning I use and on that list is a task title relationship building. I use that to send out a thank you text, or some sort of gratitude or appreciation communication be it text call, email, snail mail card or letter. Scripture verse; motivational quotes anything to let that individual know I am thinking of them and that they are important to me. That is just what I do and maybe you do something similar or something more fitting to you and that is fine. As long as you do something with some sort of frequency that strengthens the foundation of those that have been and will continue to be critical to your success.

Tools for Analysis:

3) Self-Competencies Analysis:

Communication	Software	Management	Date
1	4	5	

This is one you should be doing at least once per year to track your own growth. This is geared to you and only you. With the skillsets that you feel are critical to your career path. If done right and you are absolutely honest with yourself, you will be able to benchmark your real level of function within each core competency and from this you can build a training plan to enhance and strengthen your overall rating. Real META type growth.

RESULTS: ____

OF CRITICAL IMPORTANCE*

Always have someone you can talk to about any situation, and this person will never tell you what you want to hear but rather what you need to hear and force you into taking the necessary actions. This will ultimately stave off narcissism and provide you with the humility, maturity and wisdom needed to become a META Leader. The benefit on a mental/Judgment level can be applied as follows: If you would feel comfortable bringing someone around this key individual then they are ok, if not then you already have you answer and the time to cut it off is now.

PERSONAL NOTE:

I had that one person and he was the greatest individual I have ever met. Super intelligent, super pragmatic and had the level of respect from me that it would take the space shuttle for any other human being to attain. His name was Arthur John Stattelman and he was my grandfather. Find your people!

CONTEXT:

"It aint what you know, it's what you can prove"

A lot of people out there know a lot of things about a lot of stuff. That's fantastic, but as a leader and specifically a META Leader it's about the results you produce. How you produce them and can you continue to do it.

HOW TO:

Look at you resume, pull your school transcripts. Look at files and projects or programs form your past employers or assignments. Pull up seminars, lectures and conferences you attended. List out good/shoddy work and social experiences that gave you the sense of direction and understanding you have now. Write as much down as possible. List out what your strengths really are based on what you have listed. Trust me you will be surprised to find that you know more than you think. But calm down this is not an ego stroke. Now compare these to others that you may have seen, read or heard about. This is a great exercise in humility.

No one is 100% of everything 100% of the time so take solace in that. If you don't really know what you have then how will you ever figure out what you need in order to accomplish what you must.

RESULTS: ______________________________

OF CRITICAL IMPORTANCE*

What you know now got you to where you are, but it will never be enough the way technology adapts and evolves. You need to have a voracious appetite for reading and learning. It literally has to become an obsession. Once you get to this point you are well on your way to META leadership and you will be able to read a book, article or blog post. Take a class, course or VTM and immediately gain knowledge of what to do or what not to do and that time will never be wasted but yet invested into yourself ultimately making you better.

PERSONAL NOTE:

Everyone knows a lot about a lot, some of us just know more useful, helpful things than others.

(Bonus)ANSWERS YOU HAVE TO HAVE:

- What impact are you here to have on your organization?
- What is your total addressable market?
- What is your market share?
- What are your margins per offering?
- What is the lifetime value of a customer?
- What does your organization excel at?
- What are your end to end transaction processes for client acquisition?
- What is your process for client onboarding?
- What is the payback period for client acquisition?
- What are your KPI's and how do you disseminate them?
- What are you doing to future-proof our offerings?
- What specific value do you bring clients?
- What certifications, classes, and boot camps have you taken and passed in the last 12 months?
- What contributions have you made that generated value?
- What mistakes have you made and what have you done to ensure they do not get repeated by anyone else in your organization?

- What new tools or applications have you become familiar with in the last 12 months?
- Who else benefits from your success?
- Who else is impacted adversely by your failures?
- Do you take the time to meet with and LISTEN to your staff often?
- Are you focused on organizational growth or politics?
- If you were your own competition what would you do to beat you? *Love this one*
- What does actionable information resemble to you?
- What is it they (clients/staff) need versus what will make the greatest positive impact?
- Are you fighting with the right weapons/tools?
- What else can you do?
- What have you not done yet and why?

These are just a few questions in no certain order, to get the wheels spinning in the right direction.

SUMMARY

In summation....

I tried to put as much content into this book as possible but still keeping it a very short read, out of respect for your time. The design is not to be a textbook but more of a quick reference to get a strategy or method and implement it all the while growing your knowledge of your organization and your industry. Your power is in your processes. The processes of an organization will either make or break it. A META Leader recognizes this and not only facilitates but drives it. Any successful entity has a way that it operates that makes it better, faster, of higher quality, more successful. This is inherently based on the leaders and the function of their staff. Keep this in mind every day you engage your team, staff or crew. Do what it takes to help the form, document and continue to refine their process. The shift will be dramatic and prove most beneficial throughout. In this section I covered the importance of processes, their optimization, getting staff buy-in, support, mock transactions and Run Books. The people you are in charge of should be stuck in your head to the point that you can make assessments and decisions on who to assign what as well as who is the most viable point of contact for any given question. The features of the services you offer or products you build and deploy should be able to roll off your tongue with the ease of the name of your significant other. This is the starting point for any and all improvements, if you don't know what you have and where it is deficient then you have no clue where to begin to fix it. On the other hand, if you know what you have and you have identified why it works as well as it does, you now have that as a template to use elsewhere in your organization to improve those deficiencies and leverage what has been proven. You have to take stock before you can know what direction to go. That is the beginnings of a META leader one that is about to lift his organization to an entirely new elevation.

"A rising tide raises all boats"

The next Book will address Future State (Creating the future) and what you can do to adequately plan and prepare for the initiatives that will move you forward following that will be the final book in the series Bridging the Gap (META Execution reroute to tomorrow) . Keep in mind that a META leader is the hardest worker, the effort required is not for everyone. The constant learning, growing both as a planner, technical expert as well as a great communicator is taxing. In the end it is worth it not just to the organizations you work for but to yourself and those you care most about.

IN CASE YOU MISSED THEM:

The following are the basic strategies listed in this book. In case you skimmed passed them or ran straight to the back for a quick and dirty.

1) Identify, Isolate, Breakdown and document all of the processes for all of the output you are responsible for. Your goal should be to know everything about everything. Will you reach this, Maybe, maybe not but the more you do know the more you can do and the more you are prepared for. Know what all the inputs are, what each costs and how much time it takes from start to finish for each one. Whether you use a flowchart, Word document or your organization has a standardized documentation process, get as much information as possible.
2) Identify any Single points of failure that expose the process to any risks, be they delays, cost overruns, and or defects. Include these as well in your documentation.
3) To get time you must give time. Do not waste your time or that of others, no further explanation needed.

4) Have conversations; constantly be on the lookout for individuals in the know. Sales, Contacts, Promotions, Raises and bonuses are all tied to the number of conversations you do or do not have. Look for opportunities because they will never come looking for you. Keep track of these as well. To have control of "Your Own" data should be a foregone conclusion.
5) Never, ever stop learning. Technology never stops advancing and by the transitive properties, neither can you. Take classes, teach classes, attend and give seminars, webinars etc.
6) Be the example, a true META leader is the example, this person is the one everyone runs to in an emergency because they have the answers (Or at least know where to get them). Always professional, articulate, and in charge of whatever situation they are placed in. A META is a problem solver, a strategist and tactician simultaneously.
7) You are the most important part of this path, none of this works if you don't. The amount of effort necessary should not be taken lightly. Nothing can put in the effort for you. If you think it's going to take a day, schedule a week. Do this to give you the time to go further and put in

the same consistent effort minute by minute, day by day. Then over time while minimizing burnout. Be open, Be approachable, ALWAYS BE ON YOUR GAME! Remember every minute you are not pushing forward, someone else is and they are coming for everything you have. It's predatory but its nature. Ask the taxi companies if they saw UBER coming?

POSTSCRIPT

Ultimately I would like to thank you for taking time to not only read my words but put your resources into getting better. We live in a world of convenience and complacency. A world where people are more concerned with being right "Factually" Than doing what's right. As a leader you have an obligation to Sheppard your organization, people and self in a manner that advances the good of all. The strategies, tactics and methodologies in this text have been assimilated over years of work in IT across a multitude of industries and companies ranging from start-up to Fortune 500. I tried to present them in a very concise fashion while providing enough depth to introduce them adequately. My intent was to provide enough guidance that anyone could take over a leadership position in Information Technology and hit the ground running without a doubt that these methods would prove profitable, adaptable and sustainable simultaneously.

My name is J. Michael Stattelman from one professional to another, I wish you the best of luck and look forward to reading about you as a Paragon of IT really soon.

A/B Testing: also called “Split testing” in web development is the use of 2 different web pages to test the acceptance or test conversion rates and compare the results, thus giving you actionable information with which to choose. This can be done for a myriad of other materials as well, ads, content, journey lines, presentations etc.

Agency Problem: (as defined by http://www.businessdictionary.com/definition/agency-problem.html) A conflict arising when people (the agents) entrusted to look after the interests of others (the principals) use the authority or power for their own benefit instead. It is a pervasive problem and exists in practically every organization whether a business, church, club, or government. Organizations try to solve it by instituting measures such as tough screening processes, incentives for good behavior and punishments for bad behavior, watchdog bodies, and so on but no organization can remedy it completely because the costs of doing so sooner or later outweigh the worth of the results.

Agile: was developed for projects requiring significant flexibility and speed and is comprised of “sprints” – short delivery cycles. Agile may be best-suited for projects requiring less control and real-time communication within self-motivated team settings. Agile is highly iterative, allowing for rapid adjustments throughout a project.

Breaking Set: a tool used to generate additional ideas related to those already defined.

CMDB: (as defined by https://www.manageengine.com/products/asset-explorer/cmdb-configuration-management-database.html) Configuration Management Database (CMDB) is a centralized repository that stores information on all the significant entities in your IT environment. The entities, termed as Configuration Items (CIs) can be hardware, the installed software applications, documents, business services and also the people that are part of your IT system. Unlike the asset database that comprises of a bunch of assets, the CMDB is designed to support a vast IT structure where the interrelations between the CIs are maintained and supported successfully.

Critical Chain Project Management (CCPM): differs from Critical Path Method (CPM) in that it focuses on the use of resources within a project instead of project activities. To address potential issues with resources, buffers are built in to ensure projects are on-time and that safety is not compromised.

Critical Path Method (CPM): is a step-by-step methodology used for projects with interdependent activities. It contains a list of activities and uses a work-break-down structure (WBS), a timeline to complete and dependencies, milestones and deliverables. It outlines critical and non-critical activities by calculating the "longest" (on the critical path) and "shortest" (float) time to complete tasks to determine which activities are critical and which are not.

Functions of probability: basically a calculation in decision making that the total number of outcomes you are looking for and divides them by the total number of possible outcomes.

Meta: (as defined by http://www.merriam-webster.com/dictionary/Meta)

1 a : occurring later than or in succession to : after <metestrus>

b : situated behind or beyond <metencephalon> <metacarpus>

c : later or more highly organized or specialized form of <metaxylem>

2 : change : transformation <metaplasia>

3 [metaphysics] : more comprehensive : transcending <metapsychological> —usually used with the name of a discipline to designate a new but related discipline designed to deal critically with the original one <metamathematics>

4 a : involving substitution at or characterized by two positions in the benzene ring that are separated by one carbon atom <meta-xylene>

b : derived from by loss of water <metaphosphoric acid>

Newsjacking: the art and science of injecting your ideas into a breaking news story and generating tons of media coverage and social media engagement.(defined by: newsjacking.com)

RAD (rapid application development): usually embraces object-oriented programming methodology, which inherently fosters software re-use. The most popular object-oriented programming languages, C++ and Java, are offered in visual programming packages often described as providing rapid application development.

Six Sigma: was originally developed by Motorola to eliminate waste and improve processes and profits. It is data-driven and has three key components: DMAIC (define, measure, analyze, improve and control) DMADV (define, measure, analyze, design and verify) and DFSS (which stands for "Design for Six Sigma" and can include the previous options, as well as others, like IDOV – identify, design, optimize and verify). Six sigma is sometimes debated as a methodology in the PM community.

Scrum: (named after rugby) is a part of the agile framework and is also iterative in nature. "Scrum sessions" or "30-day sprints" are used to determine prioritized tasks. A Scrum Master is used to facilitate instead of a Project Manager. Small teams may be assembled to focus on specific tasks independently and then meet with the Scrum Master to evaluate progress or results and reprioritize backlogged tasks.

Technical Debt: Technical debt can be compared to monetary debt. If technical debt is not repaid, it can accumulate 'interest', making it harder to implement changes later on. Unaddressed technical debt increases software entropy. Technical debt is not necessarily a bad thing, and sometimes (e.g., as a proof-of-concept) technical debt is required to move projects forward. On the other hand, some experts claim that the "technical debt" metaphor tends to minimize the impact, which results in insufficient prioritization of the necessary work to correct it.

VENN diagram: a diagram representing mathematical or logical sets pictorially as circles or closed curves within an enclosing rectangle (the universal set), common elements of the sets being represented by the areas of overlap among the circles.

Waterfall methodology: is sequential in nature; it's used across many industries, most commonly in software development. It's comprised of static phases (requirements analysis, design, testing, implementation and maintenance), executed in a specific order. Waterfall allows for increased control throughout each phase but can be highly inflexible if scope changes may be anticipated later.

"All glory and honor is yours almighty father, forever and ever. Amen"

MJS

www.ingramcontent.com/pod-product-compliance
Lightning Source LLC
Chambersburg PA
CBHW021436170526
45164CB00001B/265

* 9 7 8 1 5 4 0 6 3 5 9 6 9 *